SCHOLASTIC READER
LEVEL 1
50-250 WORDS

SEA HORSES

by Nicole Corse

CONCORDIA UNIVERSITY LIBRARY
PORTLAND, OR 97211

Scholastic Inc.
New York   Toronto   London   Auckland
Sydney   Mexico City   New Delhi   Hong Kong

PHOTO CREDITS
Front cover and p. 1: Rbbr Dckybk/Istockphoto; back cover: Agefotostock/Istock-
photo; p. 2: Frogkick/Istockphoto; p. 3: Agefotostock/Istockphoto; p. 4: Skynesher/
Istockphoto; p. 5 (top): Sartore Joel/Gettyimages; p. 5 (left): John Van Decker/Alamy;
p. 5 (right): Photoshot Holdings Ltd/Alamy; p. 6: Photononstop/Superstock; p. 7:
Lawson Wood/Corbis; p. 8: Chris Newbert/Minden Pictures; p. 9: Brenna Hernandez/
Shedd/Seapics.com; p.10–11: Ethan Daniels/Seapics.com; pp. 12–13: D.R. Schrichte/
Seapics.com; p. 14: Brandon Cole Photography; p. 15: E-Photography/Seapics.com;
pp. 16–17: Jeff Rotman/Nature Picture Library; p.18: Jot/Istockphoto; p. 19: Birgitte
Wilms/Minden Pictures; pp. 20–21: Stephen Frink/Science Faction/Corbis; pp. 22–23:
Hal Beral/Corbis; pp. 24–25: Reinhard Dirscherl/Seapics.com; p. 26: Rudie Kuiter/
Seapics.com; p. 27: Frogkick/Istockphoto; p. 28: Shinji Kusano/Minden Pictures;
p. 29: Noriaki Yamamoto/Nature Production/Minden Pictures; p.30: Jonathan Bird/
Seapics.com; p. 31: David Fleetham/Visuals Unlimited/Corbis.

No part of this work may be reproduced in whole or in part, stored in a retrieval
system, or transmitted in any form or by any means, electronic, mechanical, photo-
copying, recording, or otherwise, without written permission of the publisher. For
information regarding permission, write to Scholastic Inc., Attention: Permissions
Department, 557 Broadway, New York, NY 10012.

ISBN 978-0-545-27333-6

Copyright © 2011 Scholastic Inc.
All rights reserved. Published by Scholastic Inc.
SCHOLASTIC and associated logos are trademarks and/or registered trademarks of
Scholastic Inc.
Lexile is a registered trademark of MetaMetrics, Inc.

12 11 10 9 8 7 6 5 4 3 2 1   11 12 13 14 15 16/0

Printed in the U.S.A. 40
First printing, January 2011

Sea horses are a type of fish.

They live in the ocean.

Sea horses can be many different colors.

Like other fish, sea horses
have fins.

They also breathe
out of **gills**.

7

Unlike most fish, sea horses do not have scales.

Instead, their bodies are covered in a thick skin with bony ridges.

Sea horses are weak swimmers.

Strong waves of water, called **currents**, can easily move them.

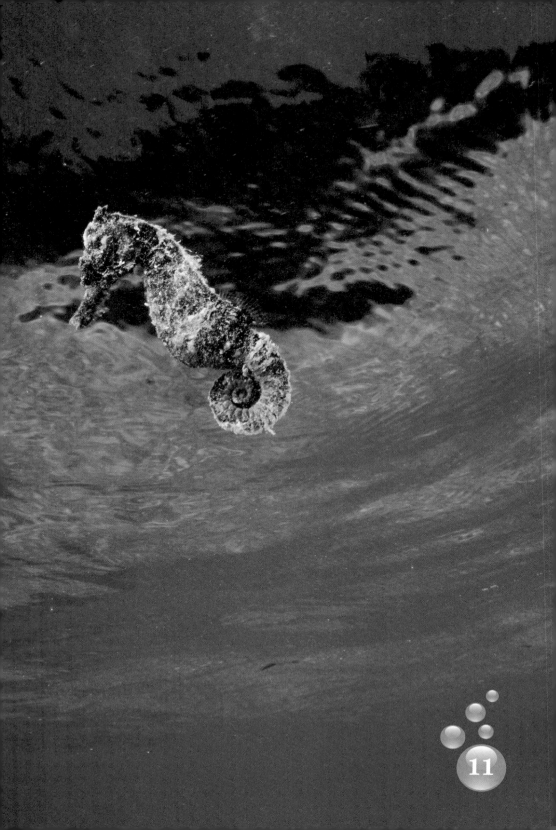

Their long tails wrap around coral and other objects.

This helps them stay in place.

Sea horses do not have teeth.

They swallow their
food whole.

15

Sea horses eat all of
the time.

This is because they do not have a stomach to store food.

Sea horses can be food for **predators**.

Crabs, tuna, and
other ocean creatures
eat sea horses.

Sea horses can blend
into their surroundings.

This is called **camouflage.**

A sea horse can look like
a piece of coral.

This helps the sea horse hide from predators.

A female sea horse is
ready to lay her eggs.

She puts the eggs in a male sea horse's pouch.

He protects the eggs
while they grow.

Soon the baby sea horses are ready to be born.

Male sea horses are the only male animals that have babies.

The baby sea horses stay close to their father, then swim away.

Many sea horses are **endangered.**

It is important for
people to protect them.

Glossary

Camouflage – coloring that helps an animal blend into its surroundings

Currents – strong waves of water

Endangered – when a type of animal is in danger of dying out

Gills – the part of a fish responsible for breathing

Predators – animals that eat other animals

C.Lit QL 638 .S9 C67 2011
Corse, Nicole.
Seahorses